TAKE ACTION!

REDUCE,
REUSE, RECYCLE!

By Kirsty Holmes

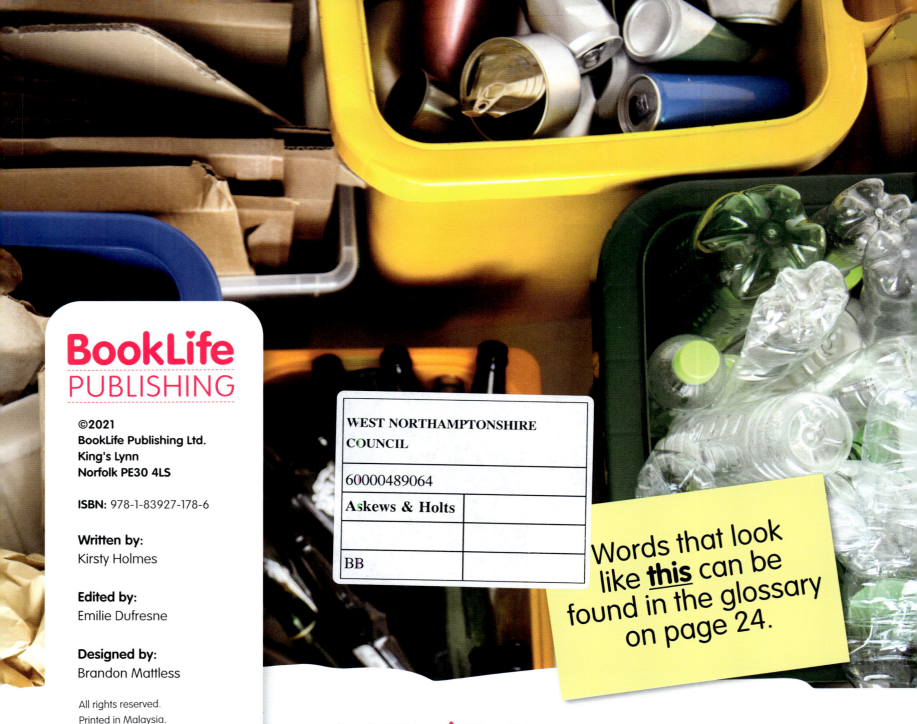

BookLife
PUBLISHING

©2021
BookLife Publishing Ltd.
King's Lynn
Norfolk PE30 4LS

ISBN: 978-1-83927-178-6

Written by:
Kirsty Holmes

Edited by:
Emilie Dufresne

Designed by:
Brandon Mattless

Words that look like **this** can be found in the glossary on page 24.

PHOTO CREDITS

All images are courtesy of Shutterstock.com, unless otherwise specified. With thanks to Getty Images, Thinkstock Photo and iStockphoto. Front Cover – Kirill.Veretennikov, backUp, Ohn Mar, lovelyday12, Peter Hermes Furian, tr3gin. Recurring Images – Kirill.Veretennikov, Katerina Davidenko, Peter Hermes Furian, tr3gin, Gil C, Ohn Mar. 2-3 – Rawpixel.com. 4-5 – paulaphoto, Preto Perola. 6-7 – Huguette Roe, Kwangmoozaa, Maxim Blinkov. 8-9 – Anatoliy Karlyuk, Rawpixel.com, vchal. 10-11 – 3445128471, lovelyday12, Ropisme, Yellow Cat. 12-13 – AVAVA, Purino, Roman Motizov, Veja, Zarya Maxim Alexandrovich. 14-15 – Andrei Kuzmik, Fotyma, Gulpa, hidesy, HollyHarry, myboys.me, Sikhorn Palanan. 16-17 – Andrey_Kuzmin, Blaj Gabriel, Yuriy Golub. 18-19 – FotoHelin, lavizzara. 20-21 – Alba_alioth, Dmytro Zinkevych. 22-23 – Hurst Photo, Ittidech, Jr images, panyajampatong, Rawpixel.com.

CONTENTS

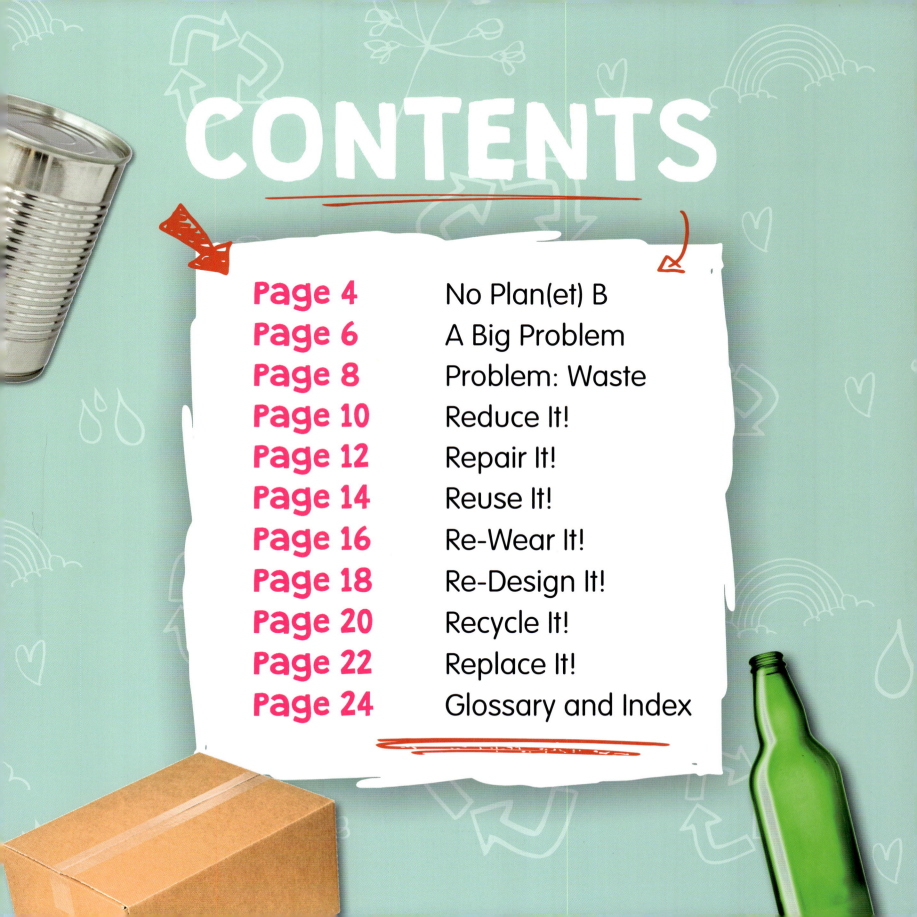

NO PLAN(ET) B

Imagine somewhere beautiful. It could be a sandy beach, a rainforest, or a snowy mountain. Well, you're in luck – here on Earth we have all those places and more.

Where are you imagining?

Planet Earth is our home. We need to take care of planet Earth because there is no other planet we can live on.

A BIG PROBLEM

However, many grown-ups haven't been taking very good care of our home.

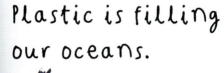

Plastic is filling our oceans.

We're filling the land with rubbish.

Our beaches are covered in waste.

As scary as it sounds, it is important to do everything we can to help our planet.

You might be thinking:

We need to reduce (make less), reuse (use again) and recycle our waste to help protect the **environment**.

"What can I do about it?"

"I'm just a kid!"

Turns out, you can do a lot!

It's time to **TAKE ACTION!**

PROBLEM: WASTE

Humans create a lot of waste. Everything that we use and then throw away has to go somewhere. Often our waste is put into **landfill** sites like this one.

Some **materials**, such as plastic, don't **biodegrade**.

There are lots of things we can do to reduce how much of our waste goes to landfill.

TAKE ACTION! Handle your waste **responsibly**!

REDUCE IT!

A million plastic bottles are bought around the world every minute. Many of these are thrown away, along with all the other rubbish we make.

Saying no to **disposable** items will reduce your waste.

BRILLIANT WAYS TO REDUCE WASTE

1. <u>Use reusable products</u>!

Buying things that can be used again and again saves waste!

2. <u>Repair</u>!

Fix any broken items of clothing to make them last longer.

3. <u>Eat leftovers</u>!

Eating leftover food reduces food waste.

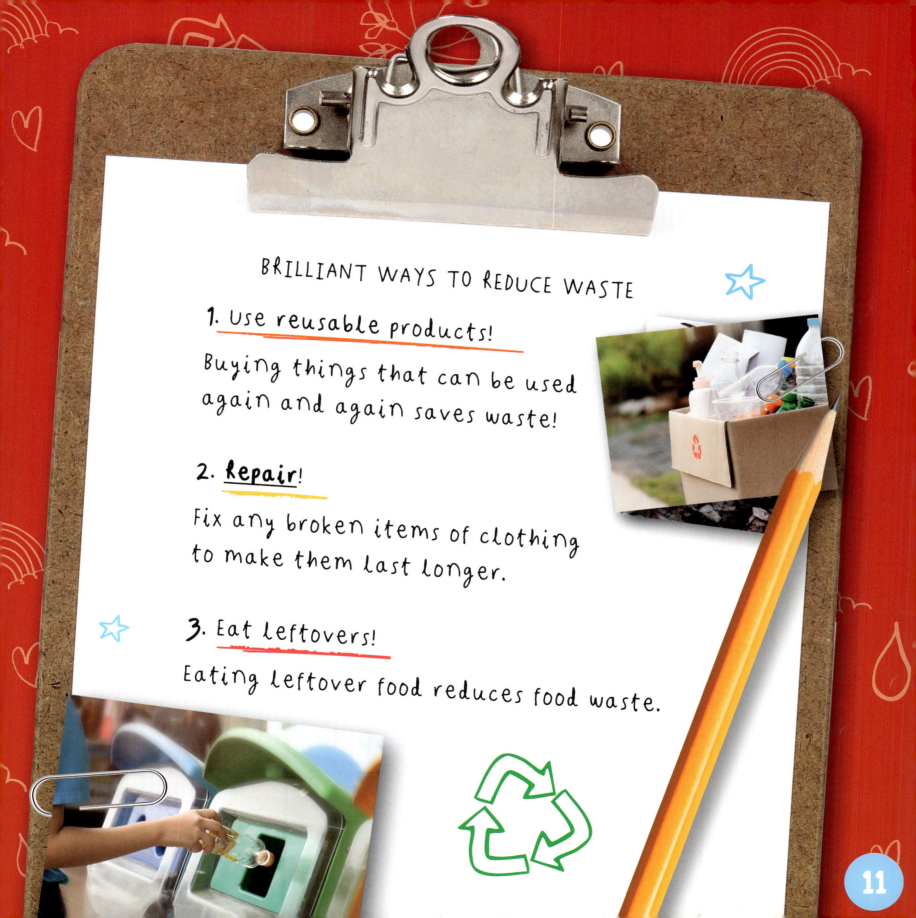

REPAIR IT!

TAKE ACTION!

Repairing things is better than throwing them away. Sort your toys and save waste!

Put your toys in three piles.

1. Toys that you want to keep
2. Toys that aren't broken, but you don't play with anymore
3. Broken toys

Pile 1: Put these away.

Pile 2: **Donate** these so they can have a second life.

Pile 3: Fix what you can and recycle what you can't!

13

REUSE IT!

Lots of disposable things can be replaced with reusable ones, which can be washed and used again and again.

Just one reusable bottle can stop hundreds of disposable ones being thrown away.

Using reusable items will save money and the planet because you won't need to buy disposable things every time.

Cloth gift wrap

Shopping bag

Drinking cup

Cutlery

Cloth nappies

Metal straw

TAKE ACTION! Ask the grown-ups you know to start using more reusable items.

RE-WEAR IT!

Fast fashion means clothes that are cheap and often made with some plastic in. Look after the clothes you already have instead of buying lots of new ones, and look for **natural** materials.

100% NATURAL

The labels on clothes will tell you what they are made of.

Can you wear your old clothes in a new way? Don't throw away that t-shirt or hat! Ask an adult to help you sew your way to saving the planet.

Fix a stained t-shirt with a star or smiley face!

RE-DESIGN IT!

Some items are too worn-out or broken to be used the way they are supposed to. But wait! Before you throw them away, see if you can find them a new life doing a different job.

TAKE ACTION! Think before you throw it away!

Lots of things can have a new job. A tin can could hold pencils, an old tyre can become a swing, and even t-shirts can be cut into strips and used to make rugs!

RECYCLE IT!

In the end, you will need to get rid of some things. Make sure that your rubbish is sorted properly so that as many things as possible are recycled.

You can usually recycle paper, plastic, glass, wood, fabric and metal.

PLASTIC PAPER GLASS

Materials that can be recycled are sent to **factories**.
Here, they will be sorted, cleaned and then made into new things.

TAKE ACTION! If you can't find a recycling bin when you're out and about, take your rubbish home and recycle it there.

REPLACE IT!

When things have been reused, re-designed and then eventually recycled, you may need to buy new things. Try to buy things that are made from recycled materials.

Make sure you choose things that can be reused and ask your grown-ups to do the same. It takes a little bit of effort, but it is a great way to help the planet we call home.

GLOSSARY

biodegrade	to break down because of natural living things, such as bacteria
disposable	meant to be thrown away after one use
donate	to give something away for a cause, such as charity
environment	the natural world
factories	buildings where things are made by machines
landfill	where waste is buried
materials	things from which objects are made
natural	found in nature and not made by people
repair	fix or mend
responsibly	in a sensible and careful way

INDEX